Preface

People indulge in various activities—physical, mental, and more—during their spare time. For me, spare time often appeared during my travels, where I observed people, the environment, and countless facets of the world around me. From these observations, I formed my own understanding of what I saw.

"Musings" is a collection of my reflections and interpretations of the external world, expressed through words. These thoughts were scattered until I decided that compiling them into one place would be an engaging pursuit for me and, hopefully, for readers as well. These observations might appear philosophical, mystical, or simply a reflection of the reality we are all familiar with.

I hope you find meaning in these writings and that they resonate with your own thoughts. I would be truly grateful if you could share your feedback, enabling me to refine and improve future renditions.I hope you find meaning in these writings and that they resonate with your own thoughts. I would be truly grateful if you could share your feedback, enabling me to refine and improve future renditions.

Contents

1. Collective Amnesia: A Call to Break the Cycle
2. Taint: A Stain on Individuals and Institutions
3. Understanding Depression and Anxiety: Causes and Solutions
4. The Multi Hued Shades of Love
5. Power of Expressing Thoughts: From Journal to Emotional Balance.
6. We Believe in the World That We See
7. The Cycle of Value and Consumption
8. The Journey from Trainee to Leader: A Tale of Two Sectors
9. Strategy Maps and Business Dashboards: Bridging Vision with Reality
10. The Role of Values in Organizations and Civilization
11. Chicken neck- Kalindi Kunj
12. The Fallacy of Perfection in Humanity
13. Reviving the Yamuna
14. Natural Legacy
15. Peace and discord
16. Causa Angustiae
17. Reading and wisdom

18.Sacrifice Revisited

19.Who will bell the cat?

20.The Power of Independent Observation and Beliefs

21.Intrinsic Worth of Humans

22.Fractures

23.Bridging Generations: Fostering Professionalism and Innovation Through Cross-Level Collaboration

24.Mindfulness and Embracing the Past

25.Reading Without Pressure

26.Understanding Fear

27.The Power of Soft Assets

28.Understanding and Managing Stress

29.The Paradox of Honest Words

30.Have Humans Redefined the Divine Order?

31.The Fragility of Human Progress.

32.Shifting Perspectives

33.Tickler Moments

34.Believe in ethereal God rather than blind faith in Humans

35.Nurturing Success: Beyond Academic Excellence

36.Thinking: The Gift and Power of the Human Mind

37.Humanity's Defiance of Nature: A Double-Edged Sword

38. The Value of Honest Thinking
39. The Contradictions of Purpose, Governance, and Accountability
40. The Pursuit of Happiness: Can We Find the Elusive Key?
41. The Painful Paradox of Life
42. Ego: Beyond Semantics, Into the Realm of Feeling
43. The Allure of Ascetic Life: Seeking Beyond the Material

Chapter 1

Collective Amnesia: A Call to Break the Cycle.

Collective amnesia, a term linked to Carl Jung, refers to the selective forgetting of unpleasant memories that bring shame, dishonor, or discomfort to the forefront. While this may act as a psychological defense mechanism for convenient and peaceful living, it often compromises values and principles, leaving unresolved societal issues festering beneath the surface.

Take, for example, corruption, inhumane acts, authoritarianism, con-men, and swindlers—those who have committed blatant misdemeanors against naive individuals. Crimes are perpetrated, but justice often remains elusive. Criminals flee to safer destinations abroad, common investors are cheated and left helpless, genocides are diluted into forgotten numbers, and horrific acts like rape, murder, and large-scale fraud gradually fade from public discourse, though they continue to haunt collective memory.

This societal behavior may stem from an internal defense mechanism or a collective response to "move on." It could also reflect a lack of education, awareness, and wisdom to discern between good and evil. History is replete with such examples. Perhaps this explains why, in many developing countries, voters are left with no choice but to elect candidates with blemished records.

Even more troubling is the apathy of eligible voters. In one of the world's largest democracies, data from the past two decades reveals that over 30% of eligible voters abstain from voting. Ironically, these very individuals may hold the key to driving change, but their disgust with the process results in avoidance. Even the act of casting a vote under NOTA (None of the Above) is significant. While rejecting flawed candidates, it simultaneously reflects an allegiance to the constitution and a call for change. If even 1% of voters were to take this stand, it could act as a catalyst for transformation.

To counter this collective amnesia, it is imperative that we openly talk, write, and engage in discussions about such shameful individuals and incidents. Silence and forgetting only serve to embolden wrongdoers and perpetuate a culture of impunity. If just 10% of the 30% abstaining voters actively participate,it could create ripples - transformative gyrations from which meaningful change, like amrit (nectar), can be derived.

It's time to confront the issue and bell the cat—for the sake of accountability, justice, and progress. Change begins with awareness, and awareness begins with us..**PPA**

Chapter 2

Taint: A Stain on Individuals and Institutions

"Taint" is a situation that breaks individuals and shatters institutions. Ironically, it is often the value-based individuals and families who experience the most trauma when confronted with sudden, unexpected events or actions that disrupt their lives.

On the other hand, there are people and institutions that brazenly cross the line of morality and shamelessly face the world with power and influence behind them. We see countless examples across all walks of life—politicians walking in and out of jail, corporate convicts behaving as though their crimes are unproven and, therefore, irrelevant, and the rich and famous driving under the influence of drugs, trampling over the poor sleeping on pavements. For such individuals, "taint" appears to be just a momentary blemish.

What is perhaps more disheartening is the deluge of followers and blind supporters these individuals enjoy—many of whom even influence decisions that shape the fate and existence of the common man.

From childhood, the "do's" and "don'ts" of societal living are sufficiently conveyed to us. However, distorted values, misguided choices, and systematic indoctrination often lead individuals astray. Such people learn to live with the taint, firmly believing they can eventually prove their innocence or manipulate perceptions to redeem themselves.

But a critical question arises: can they truly return to a "normal life" thereafter? I believe the answer is "no." The burden of taint—whether acknowledged or not—remains heavy. Sadly, in today's world, many no longer care for moral and ethical principles. Instead, they pin their hopes on powerful individuals and institutions, believing that only they can fulfill their expectations, regardless of the taint they carry.

It is a grim reflection of a society where values are compromised for power, and morality is overshadowed by influence..**PPA**

Chapter 3

.Understanding Depression and Anxiety: Causes and Solutions.

I have chosen this subject today as there is a need to recognize and understand this debilitating condition that occupies one's mental space stealthily, affecting personal effectiveness and lifestyle.

Feeling low can be an early sign of depression and anxiety (D&A). These conditions are influenced by three prominent factors: physiological, psychological, and societal. Each factor manifests differently, impacting human emotional balance and overall well-being.

The physiological causes of depression and anxiety often stem from chemical imbalances in the brain and bodily dysfunctions. Key neurotransmitters such as serotonin, dopamine, gamma-aminobutyric acid (GABA), and nor-epinephrine play a significant role in mental health.

Serotonin regulates mood, sleep, and appetite. Recent research highlights the gut-brain connection, showing that about 90% of serotonin is produced in the gut. An imbalance in gut bacteria, often due to stress or poor diet, can contribute to depressive and anxious symptoms. Conditions like irritable bowel syndrome (IBS), common among those living under stress, further exacerbate mood swings and low energy levels.

Dopamine is associated with pleasure and reward. Its dis-regulation can diminish motivation and joy in life.GABA affects brain activity, and its deficiency can lead to heightened anxiety.Nor-epinephrine influences alertness and energy levels, with imbalances causing fatigue or hyperactivity.Chronic stress leads to overproduction of cortisol (the stress hormone), which damages brain areas like the hippocampus, responsible for memory and emotional regulation.

Additionally, thyroid deficiencies and hormonal imbalances are known contributors to D&A. Genetic predispositions and irregular lifestyles further amplify these conditions.Early intervention by a psychiatrist is crucial.

Following prescribed medications and treatment plans systematically is essential, as negligence can worsen the condition and, in extreme cases, lead to suicidal tendencies.Unfortunately people consider medication as a lifelong dependence with attendant mood and behaviour swings.This may happen initially,but gets regulated as the treatment proceeds.Then the medicine tapering journey begins which gets life back to near normal condition.

Psychological causes often involve cognitive imbalances that manifest as persistent negative self-image, low self-esteem, and intrusive thoughts. These patterns create a downward spiral of hopelessness and helplessness.Cognitive Behavioral Therapy (CBT) is highly effective in addressing these issues. Psychological counseling provides structured interventions to reshape thought patterns and promote emotional stability.

Spiritual and mindfulness practices such as prayer, chanting, meditation, and hobbies like reading, writing, or singing have proven effective in alleviating psychological distress. These practices require commitment and regularity but offer profound benefits in erasing negative predispositions and fostering emotional resilience.Individuals who are perfectionists or those burdened by unresolved grief and feelings of helplessness often face heightened challenges in managing psychological conditions.

Societal influences are more challenging to address as they lie beyond an individual's direct control.Despite progress in mental health awareness, stigma and ignorance persist, discouraging many from seeking help.Societal expectations, such as conforming to gender roles or achieving specific milestones, create stress and strain relationships, often leading to cathartic experiences.
Fast-paced urban living and materialistic pursuits foster feelings of deprivation and inadequacy, fueling stress and anxiety.

The increasing prevalence of depression and anxiety in our country calls for urgent action on all fronts. Comprehensive strategies must include:Awareness Campaigns to combat stigma and educate the public about mental health.

Ensuring affordable and easily available mental health services is essential. Addressing systemic stressors and creating a supportive environment for mental well-being is much needed intervention.

Depression and anxiety are not just personal struggles but societal concerns that require collective efforts to address. Recognizing the interplay of physiological, psychological, and societal factors is key to understanding these conditions. By fostering awareness, seeking timely intervention, and promoting healthy practices, we can create a society where mental health is prioritized and supported. This subject must be at the core of government and institutional employee health considerations..**PPA**

Chapter 4

The Multi-Hued Shades of Love

From the moment I became conscious of the world around me, I encountered the many hues of love. The tender affection in a mother's care, the priceless adoration in a father's protection—these were my earliest lessons in love.

Childhood brought the pure, unselfish bond of siblings and the loyal camaraderie of friends. Love took the form of devotion to my country and dedication to my work, each carrying the weight of its unique sincerity and passion.

Spirituality introduced me to a higher realm of love—devotion to faith and reverence for life's deeper meanings. Every relationship taught me something valuable, revealing a new shade of love, each richer and more profound than the last.

Then came the moment I met you. The waves of love took on a different rhythm, one I had never experienced before. An extraordinary joy awakened in my heart, and I felt the magnetic pull of an enchanting affection. The elation of this newfound love enveloped me, painting my life with vibrant hues of passion and wonder.

This love became the spectrum of my existence, with every shade reflecting the preciousness of emotion. Every feeling, every moment, became a treasure, and life acquired a fresh, exhilarating purpose.

Indeed, I have witnessed the multi-hued shades of love—each relationship adding its own melody to the symphony of life. From one color to another, love has illuminated every corner of my being, leaving me enriched and inspired.

The hues of love are infinite, each a celebration of the bonds we create, cherish, and nurture. Love, in all its forms, is the essence of life's beauty..**PPA**

Chapter 5

Power of Expressing Thoughts: From Journal to Emotional Balance.

Quite early in life, I overheard a gentleman advising another, who appeared tired, confused, and bewildered, with a simple yet profound statement: "Think about what you are thinking." While I only caught the tail end of their conversation, those few words lingered in my mind. I didn't fully grasp their meaning until I later read about the benefits of maintaining a journal or diary to process and reflect on one's thoughts.

Often, we find ourselves trapped in a whirlwind of disturbing thoughts, emotions, and desperation, leaving us confused and helpless. This mental clutter can be overwhelming, but there's a simple remedy: expressing our feelings. While speaking openly to someone might not always feel comfortable, maintaining a private journal or diary can serve as a safe outlet for our emotions. Reviewing these reflections periodically allows us to identify the root of our distress, enabling us to address it before it turns into a debilitating condition.

Even in ancient wisdom, we find echoes of this practice. Arjuna, on the battlefield of Kurukshetra, openly shares his doubts, fears, and emotional turmoil with Lord Krishna. Krishna's guidance leads Arjuna toward honest self-reflection and clarity. Similarly, the Upanishads emphasize that unexpressed emotions can create inner turmoil, advocating contemplative practices like Atma- Vichara (self-inquiry) to constructively process emotions. Scriptures like the Vedas encourage Swadhyaya (self-study), which aligns perfectly with modern practices like journaling.

Western thought also underscores the value of emotional expression. Daniel Goleman, a pioneer of emotional intelligence, highlights that expressing emotions constructively is essential for mental balance and building healthy relationships. Aristotle introduced the concept of catharsis, describing the emotional purification that comes from releasing pent-up feelings through storytelling, art, or other expressive means. Similarly, Carl Rogers's client-centered therapy stresses the importance of creating a safe, nonjudgmental space where individuals can express themselves freely.

Psychotherapy further validates these approaches, using techniques like talk therapy and journaling to help individuals articulate and process their feelings, leading to emotional clarity and balance.

The lesson is simple yet profound: expressing your thoughts—whether through journaling, conversation, or creative outlets—is a vital step toward emotional well-being. It helps you "think about what you're thinking," clear mental clutter, and regain control of your inner world. As the ancient and modern wisdom alike suggests, a balanced mind begins with expression and reflection..**PPA**

Chapter 6

We Believe in the World That We See

It's fascinating to reflect on the idea that we believe in the world we see—a world shaped not by objective reality but by our individual perceptions. Each of us exists in a reality that is uniquely our own, constructed by our thoughts, experiences, and interpretations of the stimuli around us. What we perceive becomes the foundation of our understanding, the trigger for our thoughts, and the driver of our actions.

The human mind is remarkable in its ability to process and interpret the endless stream of stimuli from the environment. These stimuli—sounds, sights, smells, and sensations—don't simply exist as raw data. They are filtered through layers of memory, emotion, and reasoning, transformed into perceptions that form our subjective world. This is why the same event can be experienced so differently by two people; perception is not just a reflection of the external world but also a projection of our internal one.

Yet, amidst this individuality, there is something profoundly unique about human reasoning and thinking that brings a sense of commonality to our awareness of the world. Despite the diversity of our perspectives, we share certain universal ways of interpreting and understanding our environment. Language, culture, and shared experiences create a collective lens through which we view reality, enabling us to connect and communicate. This commonality gives rise to shared truths, societal norms, and the collective progress of humanity.

For example, a sunrise might evoke different emotions in different people—wonder, hope, nostalgia—but the basic awareness of the phenomenon as the rising of the sun is a shared understanding. This blend of individual perception and collective reasoning is what makes us uniquely human. It allows us to coexist in a world that is both deeply personal and profoundly interconnected.

At the same time, this interplay of perception and reasoning raises important questions about the nature of reality itself. If we all experience the world differently, can there ever be a single, objective truth? Or is reality a mosaic of individual perspectives, each valid in its own right?

Understanding this dynamic opens the door to empathy and tolerance. Recognizing that everyone lives in a world shaped by their unique perceptions reminds us to approach others with curiosity and compassion. Their reality might not look like ours, but it is no less real to them.

Ultimately, the world we see is both a mirror and a canvas. It reflects who we are—our beliefs, biases, and emotions—while also offering endless opportunities to reshape and redefine our understanding. By embracing this duality, we can deepen our connection to ourselves, each other, and the shared mysteries of existence..**PPA**

Chapter 7

The Cycle of Value and Consumption

Anything that holds value, as perceived by humans, inevitably acquires a tag—be it monetary, emotional, or symbolic—and becomes a target for consumption. This pattern has defined human behavior for centuries, from the basic need for survival to the relentless pursuit of luxury and comfort. As long as something has perceived consumption value, humanity will exploit it, often with little regard for sustainability or the long-term consequences of its actions.

This insatiable drive for consumption stems not only from necessity but also from deeper, more complex motivations such as greed, desire for comfort, and the pursuit of status. Humans have a remarkable ability to assign value to things that go beyond their practical utility—rare metals, extravagant foods, luxurious goods, and even experiences. The more valuable something is deemed, the more aggressively it is consumed, creating a cycle of demand and depletion.

This pattern of consumption is on an upward trajectory, fueled by advancements in technology, increasing affluence, and global connectivity. Modern economies thrive on this momentum, encouraging consumption through advertising, social norms, and the constant introduction of new products and services. However, this exponential rise in consumption is not infinite; it is bound to reach a tipping point.

The decline in consumption patterns could occur for one of two reasons. First, humans may come to a collective realization of the futility of excessive consumption. This awakening could be driven by environmental crises, resource depletion, or a growing awareness of the emotional and spiritual emptiness that material excess often brings. As people seek simpler, more meaningful lives, the drive to consume excessively may wane, giving way to a more sustainable and balanced way of living.

Second, the decline could be imposed by physical limitations. The human body, no matter how resilient, has its limits. Overindulgence in food, comfort, and luxury takes a toll on health, leading to physical and mental exhaustion. Aging populations, health crises, and diminishing natural resources could act as natural brakes on this runaway pattern of consumption.

This cycle—rising consumption followed by an inevitable decline—reflects the duality of human nature. On one hand, our ability to innovate and exploit resources has driven remarkable progress, lifting billions out of poverty and creating unprecedented levels of comfort and convenience. On the other hand, this same drive has led to environmental degradation, resource scarcity, and growing inequality.

To break free from this destructive pattern, humanity must re-imagine its relationship with value and consumption. This involves questioning what we consider valuable and why. Is value derived from ownership and accumulation, or can it come from experiences, relationships, and a sense of purpose? Can we shift from consuming for the sake of greed to consuming for the sake of need and sustainability?

The answers to these questions hold the key to a more equitable and harmonious future. By redefining what we value and how we consume, we can create a world that thrives not on exploitation but on balance and respect for the finite resources we share. It is a shift that requires not just individual effort but systemic change—rethinking economic models, societal norms, and the very definition of success.

Eventually, humanity will have to confront the limits of its consumption-driven trajectory. Whether through choice or necessity, the realization will dawn that endless consumption is neither sustainable nor fulfilling. When that moment comes, we may finally learn to value not just what we can consume but what we can preserve and cherish for future generations..**PPA**

Chapter 8

The Journey from Trainee to Leader: A Tale of Two Sectors

I recall my training days in a leading PSU. The initial phase was all about getting acquainted with policies and procedures, complemented by back-to-back on-the-job exposure at two sites. These stints covered areas like Industrial Relations, Administration, and Employee Benefits, where we faced direct interactions with employees—often restless, overbearing, and holding biased perceptions about the HR function.

A few smart trainees quickly learned the art of handling employees with aplomb. They built rapport, spent hours outside the office engaging with employees, and occasionally organized informal gatherings. These interactions helped them realize that in a customer-facing profession, patience, friendliness, conviviality, and body language that conveys concern and a resolve to address issues are essential. This laid a solid foundation for their growth as HR professionals.

As years passed, these individuals were exposed to attributes of managerial excellence, culminating in leadership development initiatives. The PSU had a structured process to transform fresh graduates into seasoned professionals.

When I transitioned to the private sector, I noticed a stark difference. The induction of trainees was grand, and the initial few days felt like a royal welcome. However, the training duration was short, focusing on a whirlwind of subjects and organizational strategy. Soon after, trainees were thrown into the deep end with their first postings. Managers, already burdened with responsibilities, were delighted to have extra hands to help—but beyond a buddy dinner, the trainees were often left to navigate their paths independently.

For some, this lack of support led to confusion, burnout, and eventually attrition, which is already high in this sector. While a few value-based organizations nurtured talent for internal succession planning, most relied on infusing external leadership, hoping it would bring fresh perspectives. Unfortunately, these experiments often crumbled under the weight of high expectations and cultural misfits.

This experience underscores an essential truth: grooming future leaders is a gradual, curated process that hones internal talent development. The question remains: do we, as organizations, have the time, resources, and intent to follow this route? Or are we content with short-term fixes that often lead to long-term challenges? The answer lies in our commitment to creating a sustainable talent pipeline...**PPA**

Chapter 9

Strategy Maps and Business Dashboards: Bridging Vision with Reality

Excessive focus on strategy can sometimes blind organizations to the ground realities crucial for achieving business objectives. While Porter's Five Forces model provides a seminal and realistic framework for strategic design, equal importance must be given to tools like Kaplan's Balanced Scorecard to ensure effective strategy implementation.

Every business begins with an opportunity—a gap in the market for products or services. Initial investments typically focus on the core business line. However, sustaining perpetual positive margins is challenging, as Porter highlights. External factors such as changing government policies, evolving customer bases, or breakthrough innovations often compel businesses to explore new opportunities.

Leadership must remain attuned to these shifts and embrace diversification into areas that hold futuristic potential and promise profitability. Those who cling blindly to rigid, unchanging strategies risk facing challenges or even extinction. Innovation, therefore, must become a part of an organization's DNA, supported adequately by R&D funding.

Adaptability is equally critical. Organizations must be nimble in adopting retrofit mechanisms to address immediate challenges, offering short-term relief while ensuring long-term growth. Sound financial planning is another cornerstone of success. A robust financial dashboard should be monitored with the same intensity as stock market dashboards, as these tools provide early warning signals and insights for cost optimization and productivity improvement.

In essence, while a strategy map serves as the brain of the organization, business dashboards act as its pulse—both are indispensable for sustainable growth and resilience..**PPA**

Chapter 10

The Role of Values in Organizations and Civilization

In organizations, we often struggle to align individual values with organizational values. To reinforce these values, workshops are conducted, value cards are distributed, and "organizational values" are displayed prominently on walls for internal and external stakeholders to read and appreciate. However, the primary purpose of such "organizational values" is limited to aligning workforce efforts with the company's strategy and goals.

Now, let's consider values in a broader framework—human values that are fundamental for the survival and prosperity of civilizations, societies, and individuals. Values such as empathy, respect, honesty, preserving nature, justice, forgiveness, humility, and more are not merely ideals; they are essential building blocks for peaceful coexistence and progress. By nurturing these principles, individuals and societies can contribute to a sustainable and equitable future.

Force, ego, and arrogance are significant deterrents to the establishment of deep-rooted values. History is filled with examples of civilizations and empires—Roman, Mughal, Ottoman, British Imperialism, Nazi Germany, Soviet Union, and others—that rose to power through force, subjugation, and aggression. While they expanded rapidly, they eventually decayed due to resource depletion, corruption, and the erosion of human values.

In contrast, the Indian civilization stands out as a beacon of resilience and longevity. Despite enduring numerous invasions and destruction by external forces, it has thrived on the pillars of peace, compassion, and adaptation. Indian culture demonstrates that patience, reliance on human values, and resistance against force and arrogance are vital for maintaining unity, justice, and harmony.

Organizations can learn from these historical lessons. By fostering a perspective that integrates universal human values with organizational principles, companies can ensure a deeper alignment between individual and organizational values. This approach not only reduces conflicts but also creates a work environment rooted in shared ethics and mutual respect, driving both personal and collective growth..**PPA**

The more you read, the more your memory reconnects with deeply embedded information, leading to new insights. I suppose this is what people mean when they talk about gaining wisdom and becoming wiser..ppa

Chapter 11

Chicken neck- Kalindi Kunj

Kalindi Kunj, the "chicken neck" connecting Delhi and Haryana with Noida, has been a nightmare for commuters for decades. While we've successfully commissioned massive road infrastructure projects across the country, this particular stretch seems to defy all solutions. Have our civil engineers thrown up their hands, unable to find an innovative fix? Just the other day, I overheard a frustrated two-wheeler commuter exclaim, "Why can't we have a non-stop flyover that takes us directly to the bridge?"

Urban development authorities may cite countless reasons for this quagmire, reasons familiar to regular commuters. However, they often avoid mentioning the political factors that raise jurisdictional issues and lead to policy paralysis. It defies logic that an issue affecting all of the NCR remains unresolved, seemingly due to political and vote-bank considerations. As Noida rapidly develops into a mega-city, it will need a seamless connection to Delhi through Kalindi Kunj. For goodness' sake, can someone finally tackle this shameful mess? ..**PPA**

12.The Fallacy of Perfection in Humanity

Human beings are intricate marvels of nature, a unique blend of physical, mental, and emotional components working in harmony to sustain life. While exploring the human body, one cannot help but marvel at its complexity. The "components," "wires," and "tubes" — the nervous system, blood vessels, and organs — work tirelessly to maintain balance. Beyond this physical intricacy lies the enigma of the human mind, a profound realm that encompasses both tangible neural activity and intangible thoughts, emotions, and consciousness. This duality of the mind, with its physical and metaphysical dimensions, remains a topic of endless fascination and study.

Yet, despite these wonders, it becomes evident upon reflection that no human can perfectly integrate and operate all these elements without flaws. Human fallibility is not just a characteristic; it is an inherent and universal trait. The notion of perfection in humans, therefore, is not only unrealistic but also contradictory to the very essence of our existence.

To expect perfection in human responses, actions, or decisions is to ignore the complex interplay of biology, environment, and experience that shapes each individual. People are not machines programmed to deliver flawless results. Instead, they are dynamic beings shaped by their strengths and vulnerabilities, successes and failures. Mistakes are not merely inevitable; they are integral to the human experience. They provide opportunities for growth, self-reflection, and learning. From the earliest stages of life, we learn to walk, talk, and think through trial and error. This process of making mistakes and improving upon them is what drives human development and progress.

The societal obsession with perfection often exacerbates the unrealistic expectations placed on individuals. Social media, advertising, and cultural norms frequently portray an idealized version of life and success, leading many to feel inadequate in their imperfections. This pursuit of an unattainable standard can result in stress, anxiety, and a sense of failure. Yet, it is these very imperfections that make us human. They foster creativity, resilience, and the ability to adapt. Perfection, when attributed to humanity, is not only a fallacy but also a dangerous illusion that undermines the value of individuality and authenticity.

Acknowledging and embracing imperfection can lead to a more compassionate and understanding society. When we recognize that everyone has flaws, we become less judgmental and more empathetic. It is through shared vulnerabilities that connections are forged, and communities are strengthened. By celebrating resilience over flawlessness, we shift the focus from an unattainable ideal to the real and meaningful journey of growth.

The fallacy of perfection in humanity reminds us of the beauty in imperfection. Life's true richness lies in its unpredictability, in the lessons learned from failures, and in the triumphs that emerge from struggle. Instead of striving for an illusion of perfection, let us embrace our shared flaws and appreciate the unique tapestry of strengths and weaknesses that define us all. In doing so, we not only accept ourselves but also create a world that values authenticity, growth, and the enduring spirit of humanity..**PPA**

Chapter 13

Reviving the Yamuna

As India strives to establish itself as a global economic powerhouse, it is essential for Delhi to emerge as a model city that can attract both tourists and economic investments. However, is this aspiration reflected in reality? A closer look at the Yamuna River provides a revealing case study.

In cities around the world, rivers such as the Thames, Hudson, Brisbane, Danube, Kamo, and Kimmat have become symbols of cleanliness, landscape beauty, and cultural significance. They enhance the appeal of these cities, not only in terms of their natural beauty but also in fostering a positive atmosphere through the behavior of people, tourist activities, and urban planning.

Why, then, does our own Yamuna—revered as the daughter of Surya and sister of Yama, deeply connected with Mathura and Vrindavan, where Lord Krishna once tamed the serpent Kaliya—flow in such a shameful state through the capital of our great nation? A quick search reveals that Delhi's annual budget for the Yamuna's cleaning and maintenance runs into thousands of crores. Additionally, the Namami Gange program, along with bodies such as the CPCB, DJB, DDA, SPCB, and the Municipal Corporation, allocate significant manpower and resources towards its upkeep. Yet, the Yamuna remains a stark example of urban neglect and mismanagement.

The issues extend beyond overpopulation. The persistent challenges of apathy, corruption, political interference, industrial pollution, and indiscriminate waste dumping continue to deprive Delhi of a clean, vibrant, and sacred riverfront. The question remains: will the drive for a rejuvenated Yamuna start now, or will we pass this mess to future generations?..**PPA**

Chapter 14

Natural Legacy

Those who disregard nature often operate under the subconscious belief that up above, God—the Creator, Preserver, and Destroyer—will inevitably set things right. They assume that their actions, no matter how detrimental to the environment, can be absolved by divine intervention. To them, offering gold, milk, charity, and other tributes becomes a symbolic way of appeasing the divine, a gesture of repentance that costs them only a fraction of the wealth accumulated through the exploitation of nature. This mindset, tragically, leaves them devoid of guilt and accountability, enabling the continued plundering of natural resources in the pursuit of wealth and material possessions.

This way of thinking overlooks a crucial truth: the inter-connectedness of all life on Earth. Nature is not a separate entity that can be manipulated and discarded at will. It is the very foundation of our existence, a delicate system that sustains life in its myriad forms. By exploiting it recklessly, humanity not only jeopardizes the planet but also its own survival. The air we breathe, the water we drink, and the food we eat—all are gifts of nature, irreplaceable and finite. To assume that these gifts will always be available, regardless of our actions, is a grave mistake.

Equally important is the legacy we leave behind. Life may end with each individual, but the impact of our actions ripples through time, shaping the world for generations to come. The choices we make today determine the quality of life for future inhabitants of this planet. Will we leave them a world teeming with life, where clean air, pure water, and fertile soil are abundant? Or will we leave them a barren wasteland, devoid of the natural beauty and resources that once defined Earth?

The legacy of unchecked exploitation is already visible. Melting glaciers, rising sea levels, deforestation, and the extinction of countless species serve as grim reminders of humanity's destructive impact. These changes are not merely environmental issues; they are moral challenges that question the very essence of our humanity. Can we, as stewards of this planet, continue to ignore the consequences of our actions? Or will we take responsibility for preserving the natural world?

It is time to shift our perspective from short-term gain to long-term sustainability. This requires more than token gestures or symbolic offerings; it demands meaningful action. Planting trees, reducing waste, conserving energy, and advocating for policies that protect the environment are steps that each of us can take. Education and awareness are equally vital, for they empower future generations to value and protect the natural world.

Remember, nature's capacity for renewal is immense, but not infinite. Once certain thresholds are crossed, the damage becomes irreversible. It is our collective responsibility to ensure that we do not push nature beyond these limits. By living in harmony with the Earth, we honor not only the Creator but also the generations yet to come.

Let us strive to leave behind a legacy of stewardship, not exploitation. In doing so, we secure a future where humanity and nature coexist, thriving together in a balance that benefits all. For in the end, the greatest offering we can make to the divine is to cherish and protect the natural world entrusted to our care..**PPA**

Chapter 15

Peace and discord

There is discord in the world, and from this chaos arises an undeniable yearning for peace. Conflict, whether global or personal, seems to be an eternal companion of human existence. But amidst the noise of discord, we are compelled to ask a profound question—can the world ever reach a state of lasting peace where discord fades into insignificance?

History tells us that humanity has always oscillated between conflict and reconciliation, between division and unity. Wars have ended only for new tensions to arise, and treaties have been signed only to be broken. It seems that discord is woven into the very fabric of our societies, yet so is the hope for peace.

The answer to this dilemma lies not just in diplomacy or policy but in the hearts and minds of individuals. It requires a collective shift in our perspectives—toward empathy, understanding, and a willingness to prioritize harmony over division.

Is peace a utopian dream, or is it a goal we can work toward, one small action at a time?

Reflect on this. Perhaps peace doesn't mean the total absence of discord but rather the ability to rise above it, to let our better instincts guide us, and to find unity in our diversity.

The question remains, and the journey toward the answer is one we must all take together..**PPA**

Chapter 16

Causa Angustiae

These days, phrases like "Don't judge me," or "Don't be judgmental" echo frequently in our conversations. They seem almost reflexive, used as shields against criticism or discomfort. But as I hear them, I can't help but wonder—do people truly consider the meaning and weight behind these words?

Judgment, in its purest sense, arises from a reasoned exchange of ideas, a thoughtful evaluation based on shared understanding and context. It involves listening, questioning, and considering multiple perspectives before arriving at a conclusion. Yet, in many instances today, these retorts—"Don't judge me" or "Don't be judgmental"—appear to lack such depth. They often seem less like an invitation to dialogue and more like a barrier to introspection.

This shift in how we perceive and use the concept of judgment warrants a closer look. Has the term 'judgmental' taken on a new life, one that skews its meaning? In our rush to avoid discomfort or criticism, have we redefined the term to mean any expression of disagreement or critique? If so, we risk eroding the value of genuine judgment—a process that can be constructive, enlightening, and even liberating when approached with sincerity and balance.

Perhaps this is where the true cause of distress lies. By conflating judgment with attack or dismissal, we divert attention away from the real issues at hand. We focus on silencing critique rather than understanding its origins. This not only stifles communication but also deepens the disconnect between individuals and ideas.

A more constructive approach might be to move beyond defensiveness and adopt a stance of curiosity: "Let us uncover the cause of distress." This simple shift reframes the conversation, inviting dialogue instead of shutting it down. It encourages us to probe deeper—what is the root of the discomfort? Is there truth in the critique that could help us grow? What unspoken fears or insecurities are we shielding with those words?

Such an approach requires humility and courage, but the rewards are profound. It paves the way for mutual understanding, healing, and progress. Rather than fearing judgment, we can learn to embrace it as a tool for self-awareness and transformation.

In this light, 'Causa Angustiae'—the cause of distress—is not an enemy to be avoided but a puzzle to be solved. It challenges us to rethink not only how we respond to judgment but also how we offer it. Are our critiques born of empathy and a genuine desire to help? Or are they veiled attempts to assert superiority?

The answers to these questions lie at the heart of meaningful human connection. They compel us to redefine what it means to judge and to be judged, ensuring that our words do not obscure the truths we seek to understand.

So, the next time you hear—or feel tempted to say—"Don't judge me," pause and reflect. Could the greater wisdom lie in asking, "What is the cause of my distress, and what can I learn from it?"..**PPA**

Chapter 17
Reading and wisdom

The more you read, the more your memory reconnects with deeply embedded information, leading to new insights. It's a fascinating process—each new piece of knowledge doesn't merely sit in isolation; it interacts with what you already know, creating connections that spark fresh understanding. This interplay between old and new knowledge is like weaving a rich, intricate tapestry in the mind, with each thread enhancing the whole.

As you read, concepts and ideas that once seemed abstract or unrelated start to take on new meaning. A novel may illuminate a historical event, a scientific principle might deepen your appreciation for nature, or a philosophical essay could offer a new perspective on a personal experience. Over time, this process transforms isolated facts into a coherent, interconnected worldview.

I suppose this is what people mean when they talk about gaining wisdom and becoming wiser. Wisdom isn't simply the accumulation of facts or the ability to recite information; it's the capacity to see patterns, to synthesize disparate ideas, and to draw meaningful conclusions that enrich your understanding of the world and your place within it.

Reading, in this sense, becomes an exercise in mental alchemy. It allows you to turn the base metals of raw information into the gold of insight. It sharpens your critical thinking, deepens your empathy, and broadens your horizons, equipping you with the tools to navigate life's complexities with clarity and purpose.

This process of connecting and reconnecting knowledge also has a deeply personal dimension. Often, it's not just the external world that gains clarity—it's your inner world too. As you read and reflect, long-forgotten memories, feelings, or experiences resurface, reframed and reinterpreted in light of new insights. What once puzzled you may now make sense, and what once seemed insignificant may reveal itself to be profoundly meaningful.

In this way, reading becomes a dialogue—not just with the author or the text, but with your own mind and soul. Each book, article, or poem is an invitation to grow, to rethink, and to reimagine. The act of reading is transformative, shaping not only what you know but also who you are.

And so, with each page you turn, you take a step closer to wisdom—a journey of discovery that never truly ends but continuously enriches. The more you read, the more the world—and yourself—unfolds before you, layer by layer, insight by insight..**PPA**

Chapter 18

Sacrifice Revisited

Martyrdom has traditionally referred to individuals who, through commitment and devotion, stood steadfastly for their beliefs, enduring severe physical and mental suffering at the hands of a ruthless opposition. These individuals often faced death or incapacitation as a result of their dedication. Martyrdom gains reverence during times of war, social upheaval, or political struggles, especially when selfless people willingly put their lives on the line to resist oppression, territorial invasion, or human subjugation.We had our moments in history when such challenges emerged.

In today's seemingly peaceful society, who can we consider martyrs for their country? The answer is not straightforward, yet there are those who still sacrifice their well-being and lives for a greater good. Consider the armed forces, police officers, intelligence agents, doctors (particularly during the COVID-19 pandemic), sanitation workers, front-line laborers at dangerous heights or deep oceans, paramedics, and more. Their vigilant and tireless service is a testament to their sacrifice for the country —modern-day martyrdom, of sorts.

Yet, even as these heroes endure hardships, the underlying causes of human suffering persist. Poverty, illiteracy, inaccessible healthcare, and inadequate nutrition remain widespread issues. Unfortunately, the greed of a few exacerbates these problems, manifesting in corruption, misappropriation, and exploitation. Meanwhile, countless individuals are left unfulfilled and neglected. During election cycles, these very people are often lured by empty promises crafted into political manifestos, only to be forgotten once power is secured.

In this context, today's martyrs are those who serve tirelessly until death, while those with the power to build a just and equitable society often indulge in intellectual debates and rhetoric rather than meaningful action. This disparity leaves true martyrdom seemingly overshadowed by those who benefit from their positions without confronting the real challenges.

Martyrdom may appear to be fading, yet the causes and issues that demand selfless sacrifice still endure...**PPA**

Chapter 19

Who will bell the cat?

All my life, I have "heard" the cry for quality in thoughts,behaviour, goods, services—in fact, in all aspects of life. I had the opportunity to visit Japan and was amazed by the commitment to quality that permeates all walks of life. After World War II, consumers often talked about Japanese products with disdain, noting their poor quality. But through genuine effort and an uncompromising attitude toward continuous improvement, Japan transformed from a nation often dismissed to one that sits at the pinnacle of economic success. From a human resources perspective, I observed a complete, silent, and methodical conditioning toward quality ingrained in people's behavior. For them, quality is a long-term investment, unlike the short-term gains achieved by compromising standards. Witnessing this metamorphosis, widely documented by authors globally, is truly remarkable.

I understand that every nation has its own unique challenges to confront and its own journey to traverse over time. However, I can't help but feel a deep sense of sadness and frustration seeing roads in my own country deteriorate into pothole-filled paths, turning into death traps for commuters. Any well-reasoned project financing plan assumes the highest quality, and bids are drafted with this expectation. Once the contract is finalized, there should be a commitment to the longevity of the work executed. Yet, year after year, roads become tracks of pits, and repairs begin just before monsoon season, with maintenance standards compromised.

It's difficult to penalize the agencies responsible, as they have their own survival issues and must manage the "cuts" required to secure the contract. Even an inexperienced observer could trace the source of this problem and bring the culprits to justice. Sadly, who will bell the cat? These powerful individuals treat whistle-blowers with disdain, often silencing them with ease. This pervasive issue threatens to delay the realization of the "Made in My Country" dream..**PPA**

Chapter 20

The Power of Independent Observation and Beliefs

The more I read, the more I find common threads of thought emerging from myriad sources. The fundamental truths of life are as visible and undeniable as Newton's falling apple or the universal sensation of pain, like the prick of a needle, felt by every human. Unfortunately, our beliefs have been so deeply conditioned that they cloud our genuine feelings, emotions, and observations. We tend to believe not just what we see once, but what we see repeatedly, as our minds favour images that reinforce our preconditioned beliefs. This social framework, rooted in "seeing" rather than "exploring," leads us to process these repeated images into forced understanding and beliefs.

Even great thinkers like J. Krishnamurti were, at one time, shaped by institutional beliefs—he was once influenced by the Theosophical Society, which sought to mold him as a new spiritual leader. It was only after he broke free from this institutional conditioning that he embarked on his own journey of observation and understanding, arriving at his unique insights into truth. Yet, there is an ongoing debate that his teachings merely echo ancient Vedic philosophy, recorded much earlier. We often overlook that truth is timeless and universal, shared across different faiths and philosophies, each presenting it in a way that resonates best with their followers.

The essential point is that we should read and listen widely, but let our own intellect guide us on the path to wisdom..**PPA**

Chapter 21

Intrinsic Worth of Humans

I often wish humans could be valued based on their "intrinsic value," much like the shares of valuable companies on stock exchanges. Imagine if there were a way to reliably assess the essence of a person—their virtues, authenticity, emotional depth, and contributions to those around them. Such a measure would transcend superficial markers like appearance, status, or wealth, which too often dictate how we perceive and invest in others.

In the financial world, a company's intrinsic value reflects its core fundamentals—its potential, stability, and long-term promise. Similarly, the intrinsic worth of a human could encompass their honesty, kindness, resilience, capacity for growth, and the positive impact they have on their environment. It would focus on the intangible qualities that truly matter, offering a clearer lens through which to evaluate relationships.

If such a concept were widely embraced, it could revolutionize the way we approach human connections. At the heart of many failed relationships lies a misjudgment—trusting in a facade or being drawn to the glitter of pseudo-characters, only to find emptiness beneath. With a focus on intrinsic worth, our investments in relationships could be more intentional, meaningful, and enduring.

Imagine a world where the value of a person isn't determined by fleeting impressions or social standing but by their inner virtues and their ability to uplift others. Friendships would thrive on mutual respect and authenticity. Romantic relationships would be built on shared values and genuine emotional bonds. Communities would be strengthened by a collective focus on nurturing the best in one another.

But such a shift requires introspection. Just as investors assess the true worth of a company through diligent research, we must look beyond surface-level attributes to understand the deeper qualities of those around us. It demands patience, empathy, and an openness to discovering what lies beneath the exterior.

At the same time, this concept compels us to examine our own intrinsic worth. Are we living in alignment with our values? Are we contributing positively to the lives of others? Are we fostering growth, compassion, and understanding within ourselves? To expect others to value our intrinsic worth, we must first nurture and embody it.

In this framework, human connections would become less transactional and more transformational. Relationships would be seen not as mere exchanges but as opportunities for mutual enrichment. The focus would shift from short-term gratification to long-term fulfillment, creating a society that prioritizes depth over appearances, substance over showmanship.

Of course, this idea is an ideal—a utopian vision of human relationships. But even striving toward such a vision could bring us closer to a more thoughtful, empathetic way of engaging with one another. It's a call to value people for who they truly are, not just for how they present themselves or what they can offer in the moment.

Perhaps if we began to recognize and honor the intrinsic worth of humans, we could build a world where trust is less often broken, connections are more genuine, and our shared humanity shines more brightly..**PPA**

Chapter 22

Fractures

Don't create fractures within yourself by harboring egos, succumbing to social pressures, or absorbing external disturbances and negativity. Life is full of challenges and external influences that can pull us in conflicting directions, creating inner dissonance. Egos fuel a false sense of superiority, isolating us from genuine connections and personal growth. Social pressures compel us to conform, often at the expense of our authenticity. Absorbing negativity, whether from external circumstances or toxic relationships, clouds our mind, weighs down our spirit, and disrupts our inner harmony.

These fractures—though invisible—can deeply impact your emotional well-being, decision-making, and overall sense of purpose. They fragment your identity, making it harder to stay grounded or find clarity in an ever-changing world. But instead of allowing these cracks to grow, you have the power to fill and mend them with more constructive and uplifting forces.

Cement these gaps with contemplation. Take time to pause and reflect. In moments of stillness, you can gain perspective, separate yourself from fleeting chaos, and rediscover your core values. Contemplation is not just an act of thinking; it's a pathway to deeper understanding and alignment with your true self.

Self-realization is another key. It involves acknowledging and embracing who you are—your strengths, weaknesses, dreams, and fears. It's about breaking free from illusions created by ego or societal expectations and stepping into the truth of your being. With self-realization comes the ability to navigate life with confidence, authenticity, and inner peace.

Rational beliefs serve as a foundation for this process. When you ground yourself in logic, reason, and evidence-based understanding, you cultivate clarity and resilience. Rational thinking allows you to discern between what is truly important and what is noise, helping you make choices that align with your higher purpose rather than fleeting emotions or external pressures.

Infuse your life with positive energy. This doesn't mean ignoring difficulties or pretending everything is perfect—it means consciously choosing to focus on gratitude, hope, and the possibilities for growth. Positive energy acts as a binding force, helping to integrate the fragmented parts of your being into a cohesive whole. It lifts your spirit, fortifies your resolve, and creates a ripple effect that touches those around you.

Finally, internal self-consolidation is the ultimate step. It is the process of harmonizing all aspects of yourself—your thoughts, emotions, and actions—into a unified and balanced state. This is where true strength lies. When your internal world is consolidated, external disturbances lose their power over you. You become less reactive, more composed, and deeply connected to your inner peace.

In this way, you transform fractures into strength, dissonance into harmony, and chaos into calm. You become not just whole, but empowered—a person who can face life's challenges with grace and emerge stronger, wiser, and more self-assured.

So, let go of the ego, shed the weight of societal pressures, and refuse to be a sponge for negativity. Instead, fill the spaces within yourself with the tools of growth and healing. In doing so, you will create a resilient, radiant self that is ready to thrive in any circumstance..**PPA**

Chapter 23

Bridging Generations: Fostering Professionalism and Innovation Through Cross-Level Collaboration

"Professionalism" in organizations is a collective combination of experience, skills, and behavior spread in varying proportions within a range of employees' ages and levels. Youths possess skill, energy, and drive, which are the execution moats to rely on for survival in a competitive landscape. With age, employees acquire flawless execution skills, strategic perspective, and leadership traits, along with the responsibility to propel the organization—relying on the agility and commitment of frontline and mid-level employees.

"New age" knowledge, skills, choices, and behaviors are hallmarks of youths, which must be utilized for a down-up transmission so that it reaches the top of the organization—reverse mentoring of sorts. Typically, glass doors, physical partitions, and hierarchical attitudes inhibit free exchange of ideas, practices, new technologies, and strategic inputs, leading to a vision restricted by blinders. The horse must look straight; otherwise, it risks distracting the rider with peripheral vision. Fear of experimenting with fresh ideas becomes a roadblock to creativity and breakthrough innovation.

Some of the practices that can benefit organizations through the cross-pollination of ideas, practices, and strategic perspectives are:

Facilitate communication between leadership and employees to ensure alignment and address information/understanding gaps.

Continuous learning by providing resources like online courses, webinars, or workshops for everyone.

Data-driven decision-making by using metrics and analytics to measure the impact of skill and strategy transfer, refine approaches, and track progress.

Celebrate and share success stories across the organization to inspire others.

Encourage pilot projects with small-scale implementations involving both leadership and employees before scaling up.

Create opportunities for employees to share knowledge and experiences with colleagues using mentoring, buddy systems, or team projects to facilitate skill transfer.

Identify and train "champions" to act as advocates for new skills or strategies. For example, a group of tech-savvy employees leading workshops on new software.

Recognize and reward employees who embrace and excel in applying new skills or strategies through public acknowledgment, bonuses, or career advancement opportunities for early adopters.

Leadership commitment and role modeling, such as the CEO embracing digital transformation by actively using and promoting digital tools.

Executives trained on strategic alignment, while mid-level managers focus on tactical implementation.

By embracing these practices, organizations can encourage the exchange of knowledge, foster a culture of continuous learning, and enhance innovation across all levels..**PPA**

Chapter 24

Mindfulness and Embracing the Past

While mindfulness is essential for living fully in the present moment, I find myself at odds with the idea of completely burying the past, as some advocates suggest. The past, after all, is not merely a repository of regret or mistakes—it is also a treasure chest of cherished memories, valuable lessons, and the foundations of our identity.

Instead of severing ties with the past, I believe we should preserve its meaningful moments. Hold onto the instances of joy that filled your heart, the laughter shared with loved ones, and the acts of kindness and gratitude extended to you. These moments remind us of the beauty of human connection and the richness of life's experiences. They anchor us to our roots, helping us stay connected to the people and places that shaped us.

Equally important is the way we engage with the difficult aspects of our past. Distress and disappointments, whether in situations or relationships, are inevitable, but they are also profound teachers. These experiences offer insights into our strengths, our boundaries, and the areas where we need to grow. By reflecting on them with honesty and compassion, we can extract wisdom and carry it forward, transforming pain into resilience and clarity.

Moving forward doesn't mean forgetting—it means integrating the past into a narrative of growth, positivity, and self-awareness. With this approach, you carry the essence of the past without being weighed down by it, embracing life with an open heart and a mind ready to evolve..**PPA**

Chapter 25

Reading Without Pressure

This philosophy of balance and reflection extends seamlessly to the act of reading. In a world often governed by deadlines, outcomes, and societal expectations, it's liberating to read without the pressure of time, anticipated results, or the need to conform to widely accepted interpretations.

When you read freely, you give yourself permission to explore ideas at your own pace, allowing curiosity to guide you. The absence of external constraints transforms reading from a task into a journey—one where you can pause to savor a thought, question an argument, or simply revel in the beauty of the written word.

This unhurried engagement with text fosters true learning and growth. It opens doors to new perspectives, deepens your understanding of the world, and enriches your inner life. Free from the shackles of expectation, reading becomes an act of mindfulness in itself—a moment of connection not only with the author's ideas but also with your own thoughts and emotions.

In both life and reading, balance is key. Cherish the past, but don't dwell on it. Read for discovery, not for obligation. In doing so, you cultivate a mind that is both reflective and forward-looking, and a heart that is both wise and open..**PPA**

Chapter 26

Understanding Fear

Fear is a fundamental human emotion, an instinct as ancient as life itself. It is not a weakness, as society often portrays it, but a natural and essential response to perceived threats, helping us navigate challenges and uncertainties. Fear serves as a survival mechanism, alerting us to danger and prompting action. Yet, in our complex modern lives, fear often extends beyond physical threats, manifesting in forms that are harder to define and overcome.

Fear frequently arises from the unknown—the uncertainty of inexperienced situations, the fragile nature of the human body, the potential for loss, or an unpredictable and hostile external environment. These fears, though natural, can feel overwhelming, paralyzing us or leading us down paths that offer temporary relief but no lasting solution.

When confronted with fear, people often cope in one of two ways: through addiction or through extreme devotion to external forces.

Addiction, in its many forms—whether substance abuse, distractions, or compulsive behaviors—numbs the senses, offering a fleeting escape from the discomfort of fear. On the other hand, extreme devotion to an external force, whether religious, ideological, or otherwise, can provide a sense of control and hope, albeit at the risk of outsourcing personal responsibility. While these strategies may offer short-term solace, they do not address the root causes of fear, nor do they cultivate true resilience.

A better approach to fear is to confront it with acceptance and preparation. Acknowledge fear for what it is—a signal, not a verdict. Accept that life inherently involves risks, uncertainties, and challenges. Instead of resisting or avoiding fear, use it as an opportunity to grow. Explore its origins: Is it rooted in ignorance, a lack of preparedness, or past experiences? By understanding the source of your fear, you can begin to dismantle its power over you.

Equally important is having a plan to deal with fear. This doesn't mean eliminating all risks—an impossible task—but equipping yourself with the tools, mindset, and strategies to navigate them effectively. Build knowledge to demystify the unknown. Strengthen your body and mind to face physical and emotional challenges. Cultivate a support network of trusted individuals who can provide guidance and encouragement. And most importantly, nurture self-belief—the conviction that you have the inner strength to endure and overcome.

Overcoming fear doesn't mean eradicating it entirely. Fear will always exist, as it is a part of being human. But by accepting it, understanding it, and learning to navigate it, you transform fear from a limiting force into a catalyst for growth and self-discovery. In embracing fear, you discover courage—not the absence of fear, but the ability to act in spite of it.

Fear, when understood and approached with wisdom, can become a powerful teacher. It challenges you to adapt, evolve, and grow stronger. By shifting your perspective, fear ceases to be an enemy and becomes a guide, leading you toward a fuller, more resilient version of yourself..**PPA**

Chapter 27

The Power of Soft Assets

In conversations about making the world a better place, much of the focus tends to revolve around materialistic goals—technological advancements, economic growth, and the accumulation of wealth. While these are undeniably important, they often overshadow a deeper, more enduring set of values that can truly transform societies. These values lie in nurturing **soft assets**—the intangible qualities and actions that enrich human lives and foster a sense of shared purpose and belonging.

Soft assets are the invisible threads that hold the fabric of society together. They include traits like being soft-spoken, empathetic, and understanding, as well as actions such as helping those in need, resolving conflicts with compassion, and building meaningful relationships. These are not grandiose gestures but everyday acts that create ripples of positivity and harmony. Appreciating good deeds, coming together for human causes, and celebrating creative arts, culture, and history are equally vital. These pursuits cultivate a collective identity, preserve our heritage, and inspire generations to strive for something greater than themselves.

In a world often preoccupied with outward success, the importance of these soft assets cannot be overstated. They are the glue that binds communities, the bridge that connects diverse perspectives, and the spark that ignites human creativity and resilience. Unlike material possessions, which are finite and perishable, soft assets grow exponentially when shared. A single act of kindness can inspire many more; a thoughtful word can heal wounds; and a shared appreciation for art and culture can transcend borders and build understanding.

To create a world that values and nurtures these soft assets, we must begin by recognizing and amplifying them. Acts of kindness and collaboration, no matter how small, deserve to be celebrated. Good deeds, whether it's helping a neighbor, mentoring someone, or contributing to a community cause, should be acknowledged and shared widely as examples of the kind of behavior we wish to see more of.

This is where media and influencers play a critical role. In today's hyper-connected world, their power to shape narratives and influence perceptions is unparalleled. Unfortunately, much of this influence is squandered on rhetoric, sensationalism, and hyperbole that divide rather than unite. Instead, media and influencers must shift their focus to amplifying truth and highlighting stories of those who genuinely contribute to the betterment of society.

Imagine a world where headlines are filled with stories of peacemakers resolving conflicts, artists inspiring communities, or everyday people stepping up to help those in need. Imagine social media feeds showcasing the beauty of shared humanity, rather than spreading division or fear. This shift would not only inspire more people to act but also redefine success, placing greater value on soft assets that benefit society as a whole.

Ultimately, nurturing soft assets requires a collective effort. It begins with individuals making conscious choices to prioritize compassion, empathy, and collaboration in their daily lives. It extends to communities that actively celebrate and support these values, and it finds its fullest expression in a global culture that recognizes soft assets as the true markers of progress and humanity.

The power of soft assets lies not just in their ability to make the world a better place but in their capacity to remind us of what truly matters. They bring us closer to each other, to our shared history, and to a vision of a future where humanity thrives not through material wealth, but through the richness of its spirit and the strength of its connections..**PPA**

Chapter 28

Understanding and Managing Stress

Stress is often perceived as an overwhelming and insurmountable demon, but in reality, it is something that can be subdued, managed, and even eliminated with simple reasoning and practical strategies. Much like a car speeding with its accelerator pressed to the floor, a racing mind quickly veers off track, losing the inherent calmness and clarity of thoughts and emotions. The key to overcoming stress lies not in avoidance or suppression but in understanding its roots and addressing it with thoughtful solutions and faith in one's convictions.

When we ignore or run away from the source of our stress, we only delay the inevitable. The underlying issues remain unresolved, festering beneath the surface and often growing into larger problems. Similarly, overthinking and engaging in negative inner dialogue exacerbate the problem, creating a vicious cycle of anxiety and self-doubt. To break free from this cycle, we must pause, assess the situation objectively, and focus on finding straightforward and actionable solutions. Simplifying the problem in your mind and approaching it step by step can make even the most daunting challenges feel manageable.

At the same time, it is important to acknowledge the physical contributors to stress—what can be termed as "Type A" stressors. These may include health issues, lifestyle imbalances, or biological factors that heighten the body's stress response. Consulting an expert, such as a medical professional or therapist, can be instrumental in managing these physical aspects effectively. Stress is not always just "in the mind"; sometimes, it requires targeted interventions to address its physiological roots.

For emotional and mental stressors, practices such as mindfulness, meditation, and devotion act as powerful palliatives. Mindfulness teaches us to anchor ourselves in the present moment, letting go of the burdens of the past and the uncertainties of the future. Meditation provides a sanctuary for the mind, calming the storm of thoughts and promoting clarity and focus. Devotion—whether spiritual, creative, or toward a meaningful cause—offers a sense of connection and purpose, helping to put stress into perspective.

Social interactions can also play a significant role in alleviating stress. Positive, supportive relationships act as a buffer against life's challenges, offering encouragement and companionship during difficult times. However, it is equally important to steer clear of toxic personalities and activities that drain your energy and amplify your stress. Surround yourself with people who uplift you and engage in activities that bring joy and fulfillment.

One of the most rewarding ways to manage stress is through social work and community involvement. Helping others fosters a sense of balance, shifts the focus away from personal worries, and instills a profound sense of purpose and gratitude. When you contribute to the well-being of others, you create a ripple effect of positivity, not just for the recipients of your kindness but also for your own mental and emotional health.

Stress, at its core, is a signal—a call to action, urging us to address imbalance and restore harmony. By understanding its origins, embracing practical solutions, and nurturing a mindset of calmness and clarity, we can transform stress from a debilitating force into a catalyst for growth and resilience. Remember, the goal is not to eliminate all stress from life, but to manage it in a way that allows you to thrive, maintaining your composure and inner peace no matter the circumstances.

Finally, seek feedback and advice from experts who can help identify and address the root causes of distress early. With the right approach, stress can be managed effectively, allowing you to lead a calmer and more fulfilling life..**PPA**

Chapter 29

The Paradox of Honest Words

If only words didn't exist, honest conversations might have flourished through the unfiltered exchange of pure physical expressions. Imagine a world where communication wasn't tethered to language but flowed naturally through gestures, eye contact, facial expressions, and other non-verbal cues. In such a world, we might have experienced a greater variety and clarity in our interactions—a depth that words sometimes fail to capture.

Physical expressions are universal; they transcend cultural and linguistic boundaries. A smile, a tear, a nod, or a sigh often communicates more than paragraphs of spoken or written words. These expressions carry the raw essence of emotion, untainted by the limitations or ambiguities of language. They leave little room for misinterpretation, as they originate directly from the heart and soul, bypassing the filters of constructed thought.

While words have undoubtedly enriched human communication, enabling the articulation of abstract ideas and the preservation of knowledge, they also brought with them a set of challenges. Words gave rise to the creation of thoughts, but they also led to countless pages filled with contradictions, convoluted sentences, and debates that often over-complicate what could have been simple truths. The precision and honesty of raw expressions sometimes get lost in translation when emotions are squeezed into the rigid framework of language.

The more complex our words become, the further they seem to drift from their original intent. A simple "I care about you" may evolve into verbose declarations that, in attempting to sound profound, dilute the sincerity of the message. Similarly, conflicts often arise not from genuine disagreements but from the way words are chosen, misinterpreted, or over-analyzed.

This is not to diminish the power of language but to recognize its dual nature. Words can connect us or divide us, clarify or confuse, reveal or obscure. The challenge lies in using words mindfully—choosing them not for their grandeur but for their ability to convey truth and foster understanding.

Perhaps the key is to strike a balance between the verbal and the non-verbal. Honest conversations might flourish if we leaned more on the simplicity of gestures, tone, and presence, complementing them with words that are clear, concise, and heartfelt. By paying attention not just to what is said but to how it is expressed, we can elevate our communication, ensuring that our words serve as bridges rather than barriers.

Ultimately, the beauty of human interaction lies in its diversity. Whether through words, expressions, or a combination of both, the goal is to connect authentically. And while we cannot imagine a world without words today, we can strive to honor their original purpose: to convey truth, foster connection, and simplify, rather than complicate, our shared understanding..**PPA**

Chapter 30

Have Humans Redefined the Divine Order?

In today's rapidly evolving world, it seems that even the almighty—once considered the ultimate force governing life and death—has been rendered powerless before human will. Advances in science and technology have given humanity an unprecedented ability to shape its destiny, challenging the traditional notions of a divine order. Yet, this newfound power comes with its own complexities, raising questions about whether humans are truly in control or merely reshaping old dilemmas in new forms.

Take, for instance, the marvels of medical science. Once, life and death were believed to be solely in the hands of divine forces. Now, humans have not only prolonged life but also defied nature in ways once unimaginable—organ transplants, gene editing, artificial life support, and even discussions of immortality. Yet, these advances are often accompanied by their own set of miseries: prolonged suffering, ethical dilemmas, and the emotional toll of navigating the gray zones of existence. In extending life, have we also prolonged its burdens?

The ways we live, connect, and seek joy have also undergone a radical transformation. The virtual world—once a tool for convenience—has become the axis around which modern life revolves. Relationships, once nurtured through shared presence and time, are now mediated through screens and algorithms. Joy, too, has been redefined, often measured by likes, shares, and digital validation rather than genuine human connection. In this re-imagined order, the divine spark within human relationships risks being overshadowed by the glare of technology.

Even our most basic needs, like food and drink, have become an elaborate pursuit. Exotic cuisines, once rare indulgences, have now become obsessions, reflecting not sustenance but status and novelty. Wellness, once a deeply personal and spiritual journey, has been commodified into a thriving industry. From yoga retreats to bio-hacking gadgets, the human quest for balance and peace has turned into a multi-billion-dollar enterprise. The irony is palpable—our attempts to conquer worry and find harmony often create new anxieties and dependencies.

It's as though even **Yamraj**, the celestial keeper of time and death, has summoned the divine council, perplexed by humanity's audacity. Once the arbiters of fate and finality, celestial forces now watch as humans dictate the terms of survival, wellness, and even their final journey. From cryogenics to assisted dying laws, humans have taken the reins of life and death, questioning whether fate itself remains relevant in this new era.

In this age of unprecedented human influence, the balance of fate appears to be shifting. We seem to be rewriting the rules of existence, blurring the lines between what is natural and what is manufactured. Yet, as we assert our will over the divine order, we must pause to ask: are we truly in control, or are we simply creating a new kind of chaos, one that defies even the imagination of the gods?

The redefinition of the divine order is not merely a tale of human triumph—it is a mirror reflecting our strengths and our vulnerabilities. It forces us to confront profound questions: What is the role of faith in a world driven by science? Can humanity's ingenuity coexist with the spiritual essence of life? And most importantly, as we reshape the rules of existence, are we prepared to take full responsibility for the consequences?

In this brave new world, the divine order may not be disappearing—it may simply be evolving, its essence now intertwined with the choices and challenges of humanity itself. Perhaps, in rewriting the rules, we are not defying the divine but becoming active participants in the unfolding story of creation..**PPA**

Chapter 31

The Fragility of Human Progress

History is replete with moments that have exposed the frailty of human existence. The most recent example is the corona-virus pandemic, which disrupted and laid bare the insufficiency in our supposedly stable lives—our economies, medical systems, social norms, and physical structures. Our helplessness during this crisis was no less traumatic than the defining events of the last 100 years: the World Wars, the Cold War, Hiroshima, Chernobyl, the Great Depression, the Spanish Flu, the 2008 Financial Crisis, and the rise of cybersecurity threats.

These events remind us that our so-called advancements—scientific, medical, social, political, and economic—are far more fragile than we care to admit. As the global population grows, the cost of "managing survival" increases at a geometric rate. Recent developments in AI and machine learning, while promising, come with uncertainties, particularly regarding their long-term impact on human survival.

Issues like climate change, global warming, environmental degradation, and the melting of polar ice caps have been emphasized since school days. Yet, the gravity of these developments is often ignored by those driven by greed, selfishness, or anarchic tendencies in pursuit of quick gains.

Has anyone truly considered reversing these degradation by curbing humanity's self-destructive behaviors? Sadly, in this age of materialism, most people's vision is limited to their own lifespan, neglecting the broader impact on future generations.

It's time to shift our mindset and act with the collective goal of ensuring a sustainable and equitable future..**PPA**

Chapter 32
Shifting Perspectives

As long as we live, our mind directs our actions, guiding us along paths that resonate most with our feelings and beliefs. Every life embarks on a similar journey, yet the outcomes differ, often categorized as "success" or "failure." These outcomes are evaluated through various lenses—material wealth, social standing, spirituality, power, fear, recognition, and more.

Which of these perspectives holds the most influence varies from one individual to another, shaped by upbringing, experiences, and values. However, many individuals experience a shift in allegiance from their "chosen" path to another as true understanding and life experiences provide the wisdom to make more autonomous decisions.

This "shift" is a common phenomenon across all fields of human endeavour and spans different age groups. It reflects the evolving nature of human priorities and the quest for meaning, often leading individuals to redefine their ideas of success and fulfillment..**PPA**

Chapter 33

Tickler Moments

The gentle sensation of tickling, or *gudgudi* in Hindi, brings lightness and happiness to the heart. Physiologically, it sends signals to the brain's pleasure center, evoking laughter and joy. As children, we laughed and felt immense excitement from simple gestures like a playful tickle. But as we grow, we often forget these innocent ways of feeling good and happy. Where has that tingling sensation gone, or what has replaced it?

If we reflect for a moment on the concept of "pleasure and laughter," we realize that as adults, we create our own substitutes for those tingling moments. These include reading a book, listening to music, talking to friends, going on group outings, sharing a moderate drink, playing with children, enjoying our favorite food, reconnecting with old friends, or embarking on pleasure trips. These activities have become our modern-day "ticklers"—sources of joy and fulfillment.

However, we sometimes feel deprived because we dismiss childhood pleasures as insignificant for grown-ups. Yet, the truth remains: we all seek pleasure, happiness, and laughter. It is essential to embrace and nurture the activities that bring us joy.

Find your own "ticklers" in life and cherish them—they are the key to sustaining happiness in an ever-demanding world..**PPA**

Chapter 34

Believe in ethereal God rather than blind faith in Humans

Is it not better to believe in ethereal God than to let so-called successful individuals occupy a permanent place in our imagination? In today's world, we often glorify people in various walks of life—business, celebrities, influencers, or leaders—and give them undue power over our thoughts and emotions. This blind faith can disrupt our inner peace, leading us to measure our worth against their curated successes or ideals.

While it is natural to admire others, placing them on pedestals often blinds us to their human imperfections. People, no matter how accomplished, are bound by limitations, biases, and vulnerabilities. Relying on them as a source of inspiration or validation can lead to disappointment and a distorted sense of self-worth.

Believing in God, or a higher power, offers a sense of stability and purpose that no human presence can provide. Unlike fleeting admiration or conditional connections, faith fosters self-awareness and inner peace. It creates a sanctuary within, free from the chaos of external comparisons and societal expectations.

Why let anyone occupy your mind rent-free when you can fill it with the boundless grace and inspiration of a higher power? Blindly idolizing others often leads to dependency and disillusionment, whereas faith in God brings clarity, balance, and a deeper understanding of life.

True peace comes not from chasing the ideals of others but from connecting with something eternal and unchanging. Let belief in God—not blind faith in humans—be your guiding light...**PPA**

Chapter 35

Nurturing Success: Beyond Academic Excellence

Academic excellence may serve as an indicator of potential, but true success requires much more. Grooming that fosters inquisitiveness, a quest to follow one's dreams, and a supportive environment is a tried-and-tested recipe for a successful career. We don't need experts to tell us that indulging in diverse, creative, healthy, social, and expressive opportunities generates passion. This passion often guides individuals toward successful pursuits in life.

Many bright minds, however, wilt under external pressure and are forced into a narrow, telescopic vision of success. On the other hand, those with intelligence who also indulge in hobbies and interests often carve out remarkably successful futures. Such individuals tend to become extroverted, lateral thinkers, and confident professionals.

That said, there is an important caveat: early in life, nurturing from a distance under watchful eyes is crucial. Without guidance, there is always the risk of going astray or becoming unproductive. Interestingly, studies suggest that a significant percentage of children who lost one or both parents early in life went on to achieve great success. Their fortitude, courage, and survival instincts helped them navigate uncertainty and adversity with resilience.

There is no universal formula for ensuring a child's success in life, but understanding a few key principles can certainly help parents foster the right environment. Balancing guidance with freedom, encouraging diverse interests, and building resilience are essential steps toward preparing children for a successful and fulfilling future..**PPA**

Chapter 36

Thinking: The Gift and Power of the Human Mind

Humans are uniquely gifted with a brain capable of extraordinary feats, from processing complex stimuli to enabling intelligent responses. This remarkable organ allows us to not only survive but thrive, creating solutions, innovations, and connections that continually reshape the world. We've all heard the claim that a normal human uses only a fraction of their brain capacity, while the most gifted individuals seem to harness slightly more. Whether literal or metaphorical, this notion sparks an intriguing question: **What are the limits of human potential, and how much more could we achieve by truly leveraging the power of the mind?**

The mind is so powerful that it often appears to govern the body like a master commands a robot. With its ability to conceptualize, analyze, and imagine, the mind directs the body to act, creating a dynamic interplay between thought and action. The brain's physiological aspects—the neural networks, synaptic pathways, and biochemical processes—form the foundation of this control. While these mechanisms are fascinating, what's even more profound is the connection between the mind and something deeper: the soul.

Many believe that alongside the mind's immense capacity for logic and creativity lies a powerful companion—the soul. The soul, often described as the seat of consciousness or the essence of our being, interacts with the mind in ways that transcend mere physiology. Together, the mind and soul shape our experiences, our responses to life's challenges, and our pursuit of meaning. However, this relationship is not always harmonious. Life's struggles often arise from the friction between external environmental challenges and our inner desire for balance. Hence, the timeless wisdom of striving to align the mind, body, and soul to lead a fulfilled and happy life remains as relevant as ever.

At its core, the thinking process is guided by the human urge to fulfill basic needs. These range from the primal necessities of food, shelter, and safety to the more complex needs of social belonging, esteem, and self-actualization, as outlined by Maslow's hierarchy. Yet, beyond these tangible pursuits lies a deeper, often hidden desire: the transcendence of thought.

This transcendence is the human drive to go beyond mere survival or material success and reach for something spiritual and universal. It manifests in the search for purpose, connection with the divine, or the pursuit of higher ideals such as truth, justice, and unconditional love. Transcendent thinking pushes us to question the meaning of life, to seek harmony with others, and to explore realms beyond the physical world. It's this capacity for higher-order thought that sets humans apart and fuels the evolution of civilizations.

The journey from basic thinking to transcendental thought is not without challenges. It requires effort, self-awareness, and sometimes struggle to rise above immediate desires and short-term goals. It demands the cultivation of patience, wisdom, and the ability to reflect deeply. It also requires a recognition of the mind's limitations and an openness to the guidance of the soul, which often whispers truths that logic alone cannot grasp.

In this delicate interplay between mind and soul lies the essence of human experience. To think is to live, and to think deeply is to truly understand the richness of life. The mind's potential, when aligned with the soul's wisdom, can create wonders—not just in the external world through inventions and discoveries, but within, by cultivating peace, compassion, and a sense of purpose.

So, imagine the possibilities if humans could fully harness the power of their minds while remaining in harmony with their souls. What heights of understanding and creation could we reach? What solutions to the world's problems could emerge? And most importantly, what kind of inner fulfillment and joy could we unlock within ourselves? The answer lies in our ability to balance these extraordinary gifts and use them to live not just productively, but meaningfully..**PPA**

Chapter 37

Humanity's Defiance of Nature: A Double-Edged Sword

It is probably only humans who possess the unique ability to defy the power of nature. Unlike other living beings, which are bound by the natural stimulus-response pattern, humans can intervene, analyze, and manipulate their instincts and reactions. This remarkable ability allows them to go beyond mere survival, shaping their environment and circumstances to suit their will. However, this very capacity is also a significant reason for much of their suffering.

In nature, stimulus and response form a seamless cycle, guided by instinct and necessity. Animals, for instance, respond to danger by fleeing or fighting, driven by primal urges that ensure their survival. There is no second-guessing, no internal debate. But humans are different. They possess intellect, self-awareness, and free will, enabling them to pause, reflect, and choose their responses. This defiance of nature's automatic processes is both their greatest strength and their greatest challenge.

By interrupting the natural flow, humans gain control over their lives, making decisions that align with their desires and aspirations. They build cities, invent technologies, and create complex societies—achievements that would be impossible without the ability to transcend instinct. Yet, this power comes with consequences. When humans manipulate the natural order without understanding its delicate balance, they invite suffering into their lives and the world around them.

For example, the human ability to resist hunger through food storage and agriculture has eradicated famine in many parts of the world. But it has also led to over-consumption, environmental degradation, and health crises like obesity. Similarly, the defiance of natural emotional responses—like suppressing grief or anger—can lead to unresolved trauma and psychological distress.

The problem lies in the fact that while humans can defy nature, they cannot escape its laws entirely. For every action they take to alter the natural cycle, there are consequences—intended or unintended. Climate change, deforestation, and the extinction of species are stark reminders of humanity's impact on the natural world. On a personal level, the constant pursuit of control over one's emotions, desires, and circumstances often results in anxiety, dissatisfaction, and a sense of disconnection from the self.

Perhaps the root of this suffering lies in humanity's struggle to find balance. The ability to override natural responses is a tool, not an end in itself. When used wisely, it can lead to growth, resilience, and progress. When misused or overused, it creates a dissonance that reverberates through every aspect of life.

The challenge for humans, then, is not to suppress this unique ability but to wield it with mindfulness and respect for the natural order. Instead of constantly seeking to dominate nature—both external and internal—they must learn to harmonize with it. This means acknowledging the limits of control, embracing vulnerability, and recognizing that sometimes, the most profound strength lies in yielding to nature's flow rather than resisting it.

Ultimately, humanity's power to defy nature is a double-edged sword. It has brought incredible advancements and unprecedented challenges. The key to reducing suffering lies in understanding this duality and learning to navigate it with wisdom, humility, and a deeper connection to the rhythms of the natural world..**PPA**

Chapter 38

The Value of Honest Thinking

Plain thinkers follow a straightforward stimulus-response pattern, which often results in honesty and authenticity in their behavior. Their actions are direct reflections of their thoughts, unfiltered by external complexities or hidden agendas.

In contrast, intelligent and learned thinkers tend to adapt their information-processing mechanisms to align with institutional beliefs or societal norms. While this adaptation can demonstrate ingenuity, it often comes at the cost of integrity, as their actions may be driven by vested interests and a lack of genuine purpose.

In a world increasingly shaped by biases and manipulation, the need for free and honest thinkers has never been greater. These individuals, unshackled by external pressures, can foster authenticity, innovation, and trust—qualities essential for a healthier and more equitable society..**PPA**

Chapter 39

The Contradictions of Purpose, Governance, and Accountability

God has gifted us with the mind, intellect, and the capacity to rationalize. Yet, the purpose of life is something we determine for ourselves, shaped by our mental and physical endowments and expressed through various mediums. However, when I observe the world, I cannot help but notice a troubling paradox: many intellectuals, endowed with extraordinary capabilities, deviate from rational thinking and behavior, their purposes seemingly misaligned with the greater good.

When I look around, I find myself grappling with disbelief and frustration. Is this the life I deserve? Whom should I ask this question? Can I even ask it at all? This inner conflict often leaves me confused, unsure whether I have the right to demand better. Yet my guilt subsides when I reflect on my role as a disciplined taxpayer, contributing more than 40% of my earnings to government coffers through various forms of taxation.

What, then, do I see in return for my contributions? Broken roads, overflowing drains reeking of filth, and unruly mobs devoid of civic sense. I see people living in deplorable conditions, no better than stray animals. Many have no homes, no access to clean water or food, and live alongside railway tracks or on mounds near open sewage drains.

It feels suffocating to imagine their daily lives—the contaminated water they consume, the lack of sanitation and hygiene, the polluted air they breathe, and the dire social conditions they endure. Some dismiss this as destiny, attributing their suffering to bad karma from past lives. But such explanations are nothing more than convenient excuses, a means to cover up the systemic failure to administer justice to the underprivileged.

The faith of these marginalized people often rests in politicians and political parties, whom they hope will lift them out of their despair. Yet, corruption takes its toll, resulting in neglect and abandonment. The very individuals who once pledged to serve them exploit their vulnerability, turning promises of prosperity, food, shelter, and dignity into hollow rhetoric.

Government administrators, politicians, and other powerful figures in society are meant to

114

fulfill their responsibilities, enabling every citizen to feel aligned with the mission of a growing nation. We speak of prosperity, jobs for all, decent living conditions, and equitable opportunities, but these ideals often feel like distant dreams. Instead, we find a reality where many powerful individuals—far from embodying the virtues of leadership—exploit their positions for personal gain.

What is most disheartening is the sheer scale of wealth amassed by some of these individuals. If their riches stemmed from genuine entrepreneurial endeavors, one could appreciate their achievements. But this is rarely the case. Much of this wealth is built on deceit, exploitation, and corruption, depriving ordinary citizens of their basic necessities.

Adding insult to injury, these same individuals often seek to redeem their public image by engaging in performative acts of charity. They visit temples, gurudwaras, or other places of worship, flaunting their wealth in the guise of gratitude, distributing alms, and gaining applause from a society quick to forget their transgressions. But who will hold them accountable?

Their actions not only exacerbate inequality but also erode the trust and faith of common citizens. The unchecked accumulation of wealth and power at the expense of the vulnerable undermines the very fabric of a just society. It robs the underprivileged of opportunities for better living, while those responsible bask in unearned glory, immune from scrutiny or accountability.

As I reflect on this, I wonder: How long will this cycle persist? How can we, as a society, demand accountability and justice, ensuring that power is wielded responsibly and for the greater good? Until we confront these questions, the promise of progress and equality will remain unfulfilled, leaving us all, in some way, betrayed by the very systems meant to serve us..**PPA**

Chapter 40

The Pursuit of Happiness: Can We Find the Elusive Key?

Happiness is perhaps the most sought-after state of being by human beings. It is a universal aspiration that transcends cultures, beliefs, and time. Yet, paradoxically, it often feels elusive, slipping through our fingers even as we chase it relentlessly. Philosophers, researchers, and thinkers across centuries have pondered the nature of happiness, offering countless perspectives and insights. But with so much wisdom at our disposal, why does lasting happiness remain so difficult to attain?

Can there be a mantra for perpetual happiness? It's a compelling question, and one that leads us to examine the very essence of happiness. If we analyze it at a simplistic level, the pursuit of happiness boils down to two fundamental approaches: experiencing sources of happiness and eliminating the causes of distress and sadness.

On the surface, it seems straightforward. To be happy, we could focus on activities, relationships, or moments that bring us joy—whether it's spending time with loved ones, pursuing passions, or achieving personal goals. Equally, we could work on addressing the root causes of our unhappiness—overcoming fears, resolving conflicts, or letting go of toxic attachments. But is it really so simple?

In theory, identifying the sources of happiness and distress isn't difficult. Most of us have a sense of what uplifts us and what drags us down. The challenge, however, lies in how we approach this understanding. Too often, we neglect the most critical step: having an honest conversation with ourselves. Instead of turning inward, we look outward, relying on external sources—possessions, recognition, or others' approval—to define our happiness.

This external dependence creates a fragile foundation for happiness. What happens when the things or people we rely on change, fade, or disappear? True and lasting happiness can only emerge when we learn to connect with ourselves, understanding what genuinely fulfills us at a deeper level. It's about asking the right questions: What brings me joy? What drains my energy? What values and experiences matter most to me?

So, if the path to happiness can be this simple, could we create our own "sweet pills" or a panacea for joy? In a way, yes. These "pills" are not material objects but practices and habits that nurture inner contentment and resilience.

1.

Self-awareness: Begin by understanding your emotional triggers and patterns. Speak to yourself regularly, exploring your thoughts and feelings with honesty and compassion.

Gratitude: Cultivate a mindset of appreciation. Focusing on what you have rather than what you lack shifts your perspective, making even ordinary moments sources of happiness.

Mindful living: Stay present in the moment. By letting go of regrets about the past and anxieties about the future, you allow yourself to fully experience the here and now.

Letting go: Release attachments to negativity, be it grudges, unrealistic expectations, or toxic relationships.

Freeing yourself from these burdens creates space for joy to thrive.

Purpose and passion: Engage in activities that align with your values and bring meaning to your life. Whether it's creative expression, helping others, or personal growth, these pursuits are enduring sources of happiness.

Connection: Build and nurture meaningful relationships. Genuine human connection, rooted in trust and mutual care, is one of the most profound sources of happiness.

Balance: Acknowledge that life will always have ups and downs. Happiness isn't about eliminating all challenges but finding equilibrium and maintaining perspective in the face of them.

The pursuit of happiness doesn't require a grand overhaul of life but a shift in how we perceive and respond to it. By focusing inward and creating habits that align with our true selves, we unlock the potential for lasting joy. It's not about chasing happiness as a destination but embracing it as a journey—a way of living that celebrates both the highs and the lessons of the lows.

So, the question isn't whether we can find happiness—it's whether we're ready to look within and create our own unique formula for it. Happiness, after all, is less about what happens to us and more about how we choose to interpret and respond to life..**PPA**

Chapter 41

The Painful Paradox of Life

Paradox sucks. It's the invisible thread that weaves through most of our life experiences, quietly pulling us in opposite directions and leaving us tangled in contradictions. We preach ideals we don't follow ourselves and, with an ironic sense of authority, expect others to adhere to them. We grow up in environments where ideals are not only taught but often forced upon us, yet our actions are evaluated against the harsh realities of the world—a world that often contradicts those very ideals.

Take, for example, a lesson many of us hear from a young age: **"You must be helpful and kind to people."** It's a noble ideal, instilling values of empathy and generosity. But often, in the same breath, we're told, **"You must learn to protect your self-interest."** This advice, while practical, directly clashes with the earlier teaching. The result? A mental tug-of-war where we're left wondering whether to extend a hand to someone in need or prioritize our own well-being.

This paradox creates a deep sense of confusion, especially during formative years when we're shaping our worldview. On one hand, we are taught to uphold virtues like honesty, integrity, and kindness. On the other hand, we are confronted with a world that often rewards cunning, selfishness, and bending the rules to get ahead. The very adults who teach us to be truthful may sometimes lie to protect their interests. The same society that venerates altruism also idolizes wealth and power, often achieved at the expense of others.

The struggle doesn't stop there. In our own lives, we become participants in this paradox. We aspire to be good, ethical individuals, yet find ourselves compromising when circumstances demand it. We encourage others to dream big but caution them about being "realistic." We talk about the importance of work-life balance but glorify overwork and relentless ambition. We advocate for equality while unconsciously perpetuating biases.

This dissonance isn't just frustrating—it's exhausting. It forces us to navigate a world where ideals and reality rarely align. And the consequences are profound. It creates internal conflict, erodes trust in authority figures, and breeds cynicism about values that, in theory, should guide us toward a better life.

But perhaps the paradox isn't just a flaw in the system—it's an inherent part of being human. We are complex beings, shaped by competing needs, desires, and circumstances. The paradox reflects our struggle to reconcile these contradictions, to live in a way that is both idealistic and pragmatic.

So, what can we do about it? Perhaps the first step is to acknowledge the paradox rather than resist it. Recognize that life is rarely black and white, and navigating its shades of gray requires flexibility, self-awareness, and critical thinking. Instead of blindly adhering to or rejecting ideals, we can strive to understand their context and adapt them to the complexities of real life.

For example, kindness and self-interest don't have to be mutually exclusive. It's possible to be kind without being exploited, to help others while maintaining healthy boundaries. Similarly, honesty doesn't always mean brutal transparency; it can also mean being tactful and considerate in how we communicate the truth.

Paradoxes may suck, but they also hold the potential for growth. They challenge us to think deeply, to question assumptions, and to find creative solutions to life's dilemmas. They force us to confront the inconsistencies within ourselves and the world around us, pushing us toward greater self-understanding and maturity.

Ultimately, the paradox of life isn't something we can eliminate—but it is something we can learn to navigate with grace. By embracing its complexity and striving for balance, we might just find a path that feels authentic and fulfilling, even amid the contradictions..**PPA**

Chapter 42

Ego: Beyond Semantics, Into the Realm of Feeling

Ego must be understood at the level of feelings. For most of us, however, it remains a concept we engage with superficially, tangled up in semantics and intellectual definitions. We debate its meaning, analyze its implications, and attach labels like "healthy ego," "inflated ego," or "ego death," but rarely do we pause to explore its essence—the way it shapes our emotions, drives our actions, and colors our interactions on a deeply personal level.

At its core, ego isn't just an abstract idea or a psychological term. It is a deeply felt experience, an intrinsic part of our inner world. It manifests as the need for validation, the sting of rejection, the rush of pride, and the resistance to change. These feelings often arise spontaneously, bypassing our rational mind, and yet they profoundly influence the choices we make and the relationships we form.

By remaining fixated on the semantics of ego, we risk missing its true nature. We might focus on labeling it as "good" or "bad," dissecting its role in philosophical or spiritual discussions, or using it as a convenient scapegoat for interpersonal conflicts. But this intellectual approach only scratches the surface. Ego is not something to be boxed into definitions; it is something to be felt, observed, and understood through direct experience.

Consider the moments when ego truly reveals itself—when you feel slighted by criticism, elated by praise, or compelled to assert your superiority in a disagreement. These emotions are not abstract; they are visceral, arising in your body as tension, warmth, or a pounding heart. They demand your attention, not as a concept but as an undeniable presence in your lived experience.

Understanding ego at the feeling level requires a shift in focus. It means moving away from abstract analysis and toward self-awareness. Instead of debating what ego "is," we can ask ourselves: **How does it make me feel? Where does it show up in my body? What triggers it, and how does it shape my responses?**

This approach not only deepens our understanding of ego but also empowers us to manage it more effectively. When we recognize ego as a feeling, we can observe it without judgment, creating space to respond thoughtfully rather than react impulsively. For example, if a critique stings, we might notice the pang of hurt as a signal from the ego, acknowledge it with compassion, and choose not to let it dictate our reaction.

At the same time, understanding ego at the feeling level reveals its dual nature. While it can lead to arrogance, defensiveness, or insecurity, it also serves important functions. It gives us a sense of self, motivates us to achieve, and helps us set boundaries. By exploring these aspects through our feelings, we can cultivate a balanced relationship with ego—one that respects its role without letting it dominate.

In essence, ego is not something to be "killed" or entirely eradicated, as some might suggest. Rather, it is something to be integrated, understood, and harmonized with our higher self. This process begins with feeling, not just thinking. It requires tuning into our emotions, observing their nuances, and allowing them to teach us about ourselves.

When we approach ego in this way, it transforms from an obstacle into a guide. It becomes a mirror reflecting our deepest fears, desires, and values, offering us the opportunity to grow. And in that growth, we find not only a deeper understanding of ego but also a more profound connection to our authentic self.

So, let us move beyond the semantics. Let us feel our ego, understand its presence, and engage with it as a living, breathing part of who we are. In doing so, we unlock the potential to navigate life with greater self-awareness, balance, and inner peace..**PPA**

Chapter 43

The Allure of Ascetic Life: Seeking Beyond the Material

Understanding why some individuals choose ascetic life is a deeply intriguing exploration. One straightforward assumption is that these individuals find themselves unable to fully relate to the material world. They might feel disconnected from its transient pleasures, relentless pursuits, and inherent chaos. In their quest for meaning, they turn toward an alternative frame of existence—one that prioritizes the spiritual, intellectual, and non-physical dimensions of life over materialistic concerns.

To achieve this, they intentionally insulate themselves from material awareness. This detachment is not merely about giving up possessions but about freeing the mind from the distractions and entanglements of the physical world. In doing so, they create space to focus on the intangible aspects of existence—contemplation, self-realization, and connection to the divine.

For many ascetics, the mountains become their ideal abode. The rugged beauty and solitude of these natural sanctuaries provide an environment conducive to their pursuits. The mountains symbolize isolation from worldly distractions and a deeper connection to nature's purity. The silence, the fresh air, and the vastness of the landscape naturally encourage introspection and spiritual growth, forming a backdrop where their transformation can unfold.

The next step for an ascetic is to establish a disciplined daily routine. This schedule is simple yet purposeful, consisting of basic chores, time for introspection, and extensive periods of meditation and prayer. These activities are not merely habits but rituals that reinforce their focus and deepen their spiritual practice. The simplicity of their life contrasts sharply with the complexity of modern existence, creating a rhythm that fosters inner peace and clarity.

Ashrams often serve as the physical manifestation of this ascetic lifestyle. Managed by followers and sustained by the donations of devotees, these spiritual centers become hubs for both the ascetic and those who seek their guidance. The ashram is not just a dwelling but a place of learning, healing, and transformation, where the ascetic's disciplined life becomes a source of inspiration for others. With their single-minded pursuit of meditation, prayer, and self-discipline, ascetics cultivate a profound sense of quietness and peace—qualities that many mortals, caught in the throes of daily life, seek in desperation. This serenity becomes their most significant offering to the world. Just as a legendary cricketer like Sachin Tendulkar fulfills the dreams of millions of fans with his talent and dedication, an ascetic fulfills the spiritual yearning of their disciples. Through their renunciation, rigorous penance, and unwavering discipline, they embody the ideals of inner harmony and self-transcendence.

The ascetic's life, though seemingly removed from society, has a profound impact on it. Their example challenges the notion that happiness lies solely in external achievements or possessions. Instead, they demonstrate the possibility of finding joy and fulfillment within, by nurturing the soul and embracing a higher purpose. For their followers, this serves as both a beacon of hope and a reminder to seek balance in their own lives.

In a world driven by material pursuits and instant gratification, ascetic life stands as a stark contrast—a reminder of humanity's deeper aspirations and the timeless quest for meaning. While not everyone is drawn to such extremes, the principles of simplicity, discipline, and introspection that underpin asceticism can inspire anyone to reflect on their own path and priorities..**PPA**

Supplementary reading

Few Quotes by the Author

Tryst with myself:How often do we meet ourselves.Our life is so much influenced by events,people,circumstances external to our being that there is hardly time for self-introspection..ppa

One way to subdue savagery in humans is to expose them to divinity..ppa

Being fearless and uninhibited can make you perpetually happy.You can achieve this by embracing the power of truthfulness..ppa

Stock market and cricket are two crazy endeavors;
Tread carefully before giving unsolicited gyan on either or get shamelessly trolled.

In the interest of cricket lovers' sentiments.
..ppa

Everyone has their own way of surviving, but we all need a clean environment to truly live..ppa

It is peculiar how perception often tends to be sectarian. However, when viewed from a humanistic perspective, there is but one universal truth that we all can recognize..ppa

Becoming insensitive to pain and suffering is the worst form of self-apathy, leading to a shameful and hollow existence..ppa

We continue to search for a better life,
If only the desires we chase could evolve with age...ppa

The Balance of Needs and Desires:

When the understanding of one's "needs" emanates from within,
The fulfillment of "desires" becomes much simpler..ppa

The Purpose of Mind and Body.

God has given us legs to walk and run,

Why race the mind, whose primary role is to interpret our senses and guide our actions?..ppa

Author

Prem Prakash Akhauri is an experienced Human Resources (HR) Consultant who has led HR functions in prominent public and private sector organizations. You can view his profile on **LinkedIn**. Additionally, he is an active and eloquent writer and author.

His first e-book, **"Khayal...Mere Apne!"** , struck a deep chord with readers. Its hallmark lies in its simplicity and profound understanding of human behavior, thoughts, and emotions.Subsequently,he published two more compilations of his thoughts in the form of ebook, **"Abhivyakti..Khayalo ki Ravani!**

and **"Dhun"..Khayalo ki Gungunahat!"** (All available on **Pothi.com** and **Amazon Kindle**).

For years, he has been documenting his thoughts, feelings, and experiences through writing. He always advises those who enjoy introspection to put their thoughts into words—not merely for self-contentment or mental peace but as a meaningful contribution to the creative world.

He believes that expressing thoughts in words is not just an art but a process that fulfills the soul.